Ethnographic Terminalia: Montréal 2011
Field, Studio, Lab
Eastern Bloc Centre for New Media and Interdisciplinary Art

Published by the Society for Visual Anthropology, a section of the American Anthropological Association. 2300 Clarendon Blvd., Suite 1301. Arlington, VA 22201

Review essays in this volume were originally published in the journals American Anthropologist and Museum and Curatorial Studies Review. Our grateful acknowledgement to the editors.

Edited by Ethnographic Terminalia:
Craig Campbell, Kate Hennessy, Fiona P. McDonald, Trudi Lynn Smith, Stephanie Takaragawa

Lead editors and print design: Kate Hennessy and Rachel Topham

Exhibition Photography: Rachel Topham

Cover Design: Ethnographic Terminalia, Rachel Topham and Ian Kirkpatrick

ISBN 978-1-931303-44-6

Montréal 2011:

Contributors

ethnograp

terminali

field, studi

lab

ethnographic terminalia 2011 montréal

The terminus is the end, the boundary, and the border

.

Ethnographic Terminalia

Montréal 2011:

Field, Studio, Lab

Eastern Bloc Centre for New Media
and Interdisciplinary Art

2011 Principal Curators
Kate Hennessy
Fiona P. McDonald
Trudi Lynn Smith

Partnering Curator
Erica Lehrer

Co-curators
Maria Brodine
Craig Campbell
Stephanie Takaragawa

Exhibition Photography
Rachel Topham

Graphic Design
Ian Kirkpatrick

Acknowledgements

The *Field Studio Lab* exhibition benefitted greatly from the generous encouragement, insight and expertise of many individuals. *Field Studio Lab* was supported by the works produced from Fellows, Associates and Students affiliated with Erica Lehrer and the CEREV Workshop. Their project provided on-the-ground connections with Concordia and the local community of Montréal. Work on the theme and shape of the exhibition was conducted with the support of the CEREV Workshop and while in situ with Dr. Lehrer's Workshop group in early 2011. Special thanks to Ian Kirkpatrick, whose work in the 2010 New Orleans Ethnographic Terminalia inspired the curators to invite him to design our program for *Field Studio Lab*. We would like to express our sincere appreciation to all of the artists who submitted works for review and to all of the artists who participated in *Field, Studio, Lab*. In particular, we benefitted from our time working with artist Humberto Vélez and curator Emelie Changgur (Art Gallery York University—AGYU) to bring Velez's work to Montréal and to situate it in relation to a retrospective of his work at the AGYU. Special thanks to the Mississauga New Credit First Nations, and Philip Monk for his support with AGYU's participation in Montréal.

Thank you Josyln Osten at the American Anthropological Association for her assistance with PR and social media. We would also like to thank the following groups and individuals for their assistance: Amber Berson, Lex Milton, Neil Starkey, Eliane Ellbogen, Emma Geldart, and Solen Roth. We thank the volunteers who helped install, tend and de-install the show: Mary Caple, Frances Enedy, Carolina Garcia Amatos, Daniel Anez, Katrina Caruso, Zoe Wonfor, Jaqueline Lanteigne, Ming Lin, Aliya Kahsay, Yana Konteft, Libby Shea and Selina Antonucci.

We would like to acknowledge and extend deep appreciation to: CEREV Workshop, (Concordia University); Canada Research Chairs; Making Culture Lab at the School of Interactive Arts and Technology (Simon Fraser University); the American Anthropological Association's Community Engagement Fund, the Society for Visual Anthropology, and the Council for Museum Anthropology.

ethnographic terminalia

2011 montréal

Field

Studio

Lab

The terminus is the end, the boundary, and the border

Montréal 2011:

Field, Studio, Lab

Ethnographic Terminalia is an initiative that brings artists and anthropologists together to engage emerging research through installation and exhibition. The exhibition acts as a platform for the articulation of divergent modes and methodologies and inquiry, a place to explore what lies within and beyond disciplinary territories, and how their boundaries shape the representation of cultural practice. Projects in Ethnographic Terminalia 2011 take up the theme: *Field, Studio, Lab.* Understood as three locations, the field, the studio, and the lab both comprise their own communities of practice and form sites of inquiry and production for artists and anthropologists. Field, studio, and lab are only places where knowledge is produced, or ethnographic data gathered, but are also spaces of everyday life and local cultural production; they are generative sites of encounter, negotiation, conflict, celebration, failure, disappointment and revelation—all of which can unsettle (or ossify) discursive, disciplinary, and methodological boundaries. Works range from video and sound installations to new media explorations and technical hacks, public engagements with site-specific interventions, material experiments with textile and book culture, and sculptural responses to social issues. Some pieces represent the aesthetic manifestation of collaboration, while others form auto-ethnographic responses to forays into "the field"—both real and imagined. Political commitments, data, ethics, commerce and the dynamics of co-production of knowledge emerge as thematic concerns in the space between research and art, and the elastic border zones of field, studio, and lab.

Humberto Velez

The Fight

General installation view, Montreal, 2011.

General installation view, Montreal, 2011.

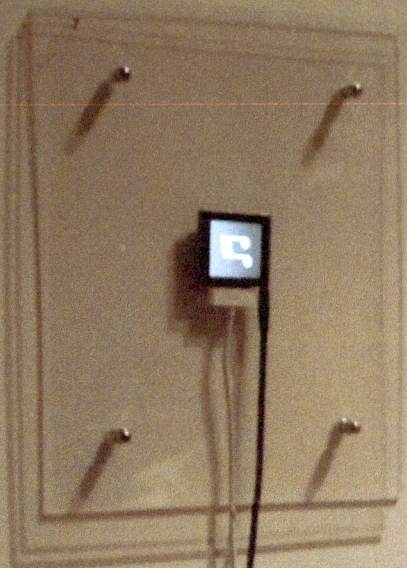

General installation view, Montreal, 2011.

General installation view, Montreal, 2011.

General installation view, Montreal, 2011.

ETHNOGRAPHIC TERMINALIA:
FIELD, STUDIO, LAB

Shelley Ruth Butler, McGill University, Montréal

Now in its third year, Ethnographic Terminalia is a popular and anticipated exhibition held in conjunction with the annual American Anthropological Association (AAA) Meetings. Ethnographic Terminalia highlights multi-media installations created by anthropologists and artists, and proposes new ways of conducting and presenting critical social inquiry. As stated in its promotional material, the exhibition series seeks to create "generative ethnographies that do not subordinate the sensorium to the expository and theoretical text or monograph." Indeed, Ethnographic Terminalia exhibitions offer an alternative to the status quo of academic meetings that rely on conference papers and PowerPoint presentations to communicate research. Rather than listening to research presentations, Ethnographic Terminalia visitors socialize (openings have a hip, cocktail-party ambiance), look at and interact with art, are immersed in audio and video installations through the use of headphones, and wander freely in gallery space.

The edition of Ethnographic Terminalia held in Montréal was organized around the thematic of *Field, Studio, Lab*. The curatorial collective called upon artists and anthropologists to consider each of these three domains simultaneously as sites of cultural and academic production, as well as lived experience. With over 25 contributors, the exhibition addressed a wide variety of substantive issues that resonate with humanities and social science research, including

Reprinted with permission. Butler, Shelley R. 2013 Exhibition Review Essay. Ethnographic Terminalia: Field, Studio, Lab. Museum and Curatorial Studies Review 1(1):116-124

General installation view, Montreal, 2011.

global outsourcing, waste collection, diasporic identities, religious ritual, racial stereotypes, traumatic memory, urban space, and democracy. The majority of participants were artists, though there were a number of visual anthropologists fluent in multi-media production. The participants who identified foremost as anthropologists were largely associated with the Centre for Ethnographic Research in the Aftermath of Violence (CEREV), this year's local partnering institution headed by Erica Lehrer at Concordia University.[1] Collaborative engagements, between artists and anthropologists, and between artists and their "research subjects," were evident in many projects. Following gallery conventions, participants submitted artist statements that were available for consultation in a binder in the gallery and posted online.[2]

Unlike previous Ethnographic Terminalias, the Montréal show was anchored by one piece: a video of London-based, Panamanian artist Humberto Vélez's performance piece *The Fight*, which was presented at the Tate Modern in London in 2007. *The Fight* was created in collaboration with amateur boxing clubs from the museum's borough of Southwark, along with the street dance

29

company Flawless, with music composed by rap MC Mic Assassin. The one-off performance involved two simultaneous processions of local amateur boxers, one led by a bagpiper and the other by two African drummers, traveling via barge on the Thames river and by foot over the Millennium Bridge, and converging at a boxing ring installed in the "high culture" Turbine Hall of the Tate. The inclusion of a series of choreographed, non-competitive fights by boxers of varying ages and abilities framed amateur boxing as popular dance and art, but also celebrated the energy and aesthetics of a mixed city. To create *The Fight*, Vélez combined fieldwork with artistic vision, researching the local neighborhood, creating relationships with project participants, and facilitating collaborative multi-disciplinary workshops during a four month period. This culminated in a spectacular, orchestrated spatial occupation of the Tate. This sense of research as a process of creation and intervention was highlighted in another piece, *The Tie*, by Alexandrine Boudreault-Fournier and Marie-Joseé Proulx. Overturning the traditional role of fieldworker as neutral participant-observer, and through brilliant use of technology, the anthropologists staged a virtual musical encounter between a traditional guitarist in Santiago, Chile, and a Cuban trumpeter who has lived in Montréal since the age of 12. Presented in a small dark room, the media installation created a delicate atmosphere, positioning the audience between projections of the musicians who performed physically alone, yet were virtually and musically connected. Boudreault-Fournier and Proulx refer to their fieldwork as an "echo lab," alluding to the uniqueness of their intervention.

BioARTCAMP documented a hybrid laboratory and artistic project that took place in Banff National Park, Alberta in 2011, facilitated by Jennifer Willett, head of INCUBATOR: Hybrid Laboratory at the Intersection of Art, Science and Ecology.[3] *BioARTCAMP* brought together scientists, artists, filmmakers, and university students to participate in a biological science lab (constructed in the field) and to create ecologically-oriented art. The projects ranged from rigorous inquiry regarding local pollutants to photographing a campy female model and nude mannequin "in nature." At Ethnographic Terminalia, visitors gained only a brief impression of *BioARTCAMP* based on three framed photographs of participants and Boy Scout style "biocamp" badges, bearing the slogan,

General installation view, Montreal, 2011.

"A Rocky Mountain Adventure in Art and Biology." In contrast, Public Laboratory for Open Technology and Science – an organization that develops open-source, do-it-yourself tools for the investigation of pollutants in everyday environments – used the gallery as its field and laboratory.[4] Visitors could interact with a Spectometer and a Roomba Indoor Air Quality Monitoring system designed to explore the gallery. The devices attracted casual attention (they did not seem to always be functioning), but one imagines a very different outcome when the tools are used by local communities with pressing health concerns and activist aspirations. In the gallery, the tools were perceived as aesthetic curiosities and playful novelties.

Sound and visual installations transported audiences to a stunning array of elsewheres: by donning headsets, a visitor could eavesdrop on everyday life in Greece (Luc Messinezis); listen to a religious festival in rural Italy (La Cosa

Preziosa); and witness a filmic meditation about a rare stretch of public shoreline in New York City's Jamaica Bay (Sarah Christman), to name a few examples. Other videos – particularly those associated with CEREV – consciously explored epistemological, personal, and ethical issues involved in engaging legacies of Argentinian political repression (Florencia Marchetti); the Israeli-Palestine conflict (Joseph Rosen); and narratives of Holocaust memory (student work from a public history course at Concordia). The density of experiences and stories revealed by installations in Ethnographic Terminalia was remarkable and demanded a willingness to listen and watch attentively. This depth was especially engaging in CEREV's component of Ethnographic Terminalia, reflecting its success as a humanities lab that fosters dialogue, exchange, and the vetting of curatorial projects amongst affiliated researchers and students around the theme of memories of violence.[5]

As in reflexive ethnography, artworks and installations in the exhibition made productive use of personal experience and everyday material artifacts. Animations of Romanian communist-era domestic objects (miniature cookbooks, porcelain figures, a schoolgirl's uniform) were juxtaposed with video interviews with Bucharest residents recollecting their past (Alyssa Grossman and Selena Kimball); recordings of sounds and voices from a Radio-Canada newsroom were used by Chantal Francoeur – a seasoned reporter herself – to explore the meaning of media convergence for the national public broadcaster; Erin Newell's poetic video made use of fragments of old family footage that documented her maternal grandfather and kin crossing the Atlantic (USA-Ireland) in the 1950s, creating a meditation on landscape and attachment; as a self-described "mixed-race mixed media artist," Chantal Gibson used an outdated Canadian history book to evoke notions of cultural visibility and invisibility. By juxtaposing a photo of the artist's mother as a young black girl with a chapter about British Loyalists who settled in Nova Scotia in 1783, Gibson pointed to the absence of any attention given to the difficult experiences of 3000 Black Loyalists. Gibson describes her work as privileging "texture over text," a provocative statement for an academic audience.

A roundtable discussion held at the gallery with local artists and scholars from the fields of anthropology, art, communications, and history addressed the tension between art's emphasis on experience, affect, and evocation and textual ethnography, which is more suited to didactic museums than galleries. Reflecting an illustrative, more textual approach, Monica Eileen Patterson's display of posters of children in Apartheid South Africa offered a succinct account of key moments in the complex history of competing constructions of childhood. In contrast, conceptual art such as Stephen Foster's multi-media exploration of early ethnographic images of American Indians and their impacts on popular culture relied on affect and evocation, rather than narrative and explicit analysis. Working in an ironic mode, Foster presented miniature toy Indian figures (made in Germany) on pedestals, and hung luminous portraits of the toys in light boxes, mimicking movie advertising conventions. The portraits also referenced early ethnographic photography by Edward E. Curtis, though only the title of the piece, *Re-Mediating Curtis: Toy Portraits* hints at this artistic intention. In response to a question regarding the exhibition's conspicuous lack of labels on individual works, curator Kate Hennessy described the curatorial team as "children of MOA," referencing the University of British Columbia, Vancouver's Museum of Anthropology (MOA), an institution that honors the aesthetics and cultural power of Northwest Coast First Nation art. By steering Ethnographic Terminalia in this direction, the curators challenged academic desires for coherency and comprehensiveness; consequently, it was not always easy to "make sense" of pieces on display. Attempts to transport visitors acoustically into "the field" were reminiscent of anthropology's calls for reflexive experiments in "writing culture" to draw attention to the fieldwork process. Many artists presented fragmented images and sound that immersed visitors in a moment – an experience – as opposed to offering a classical, linear ethnography. As a teacher working with difficult histories in Canada, such as the marginalization of black and aboriginal cultures, I appreciate that artistic interventions can focus attention on the material objects of everyday life (toys, books, photos) in profoundly moving ways. But I want art to be placed amongst, or against, historical artifacts and framing texts. Foster's piece, for instance, would take on greater resonance if it were displayed in the First Peoples Gallery of the Royal British Columbia Museum, where segments of Curtis films show continuously.

General installation view, Montreal, 2011.

A key piece, *We Have Never Been Modern,* by artist and graphic designer Ian Kirkpatrick, was inspired by the artist statements submitted for Ethnographic Terminalia. Commissioned to create a brochure or catalogue for the exhibition, Kirkpatrick instead built a fascinating fold-out cardboard model of the Tate Modern, incorporating texts from the artist statements, as well as imagery from the Tate and an array of other sources, including Pablo Picasso, Walter Benjamin, Bruno Latour, local street art, Roy Lichtenstein, and iconic landmarks such as the Louvre.[6] Visitors could open the model mini-Tate to look at the Turbine Hall, the space where Vélez originally staged *The Fight.* Kirkpatrick's piece brought home the academic, research-driven nature of much of the art on display at Ethnographic Terminalia by way of its complex intertextuality. For instance, Laura Malacart's artist statement, for her photographic portraits entitled *Parliament,* cited philosopher and sociologist Bruno Latour as a source of inspiration. This led Kirkpatrick to read Latour and title his piece

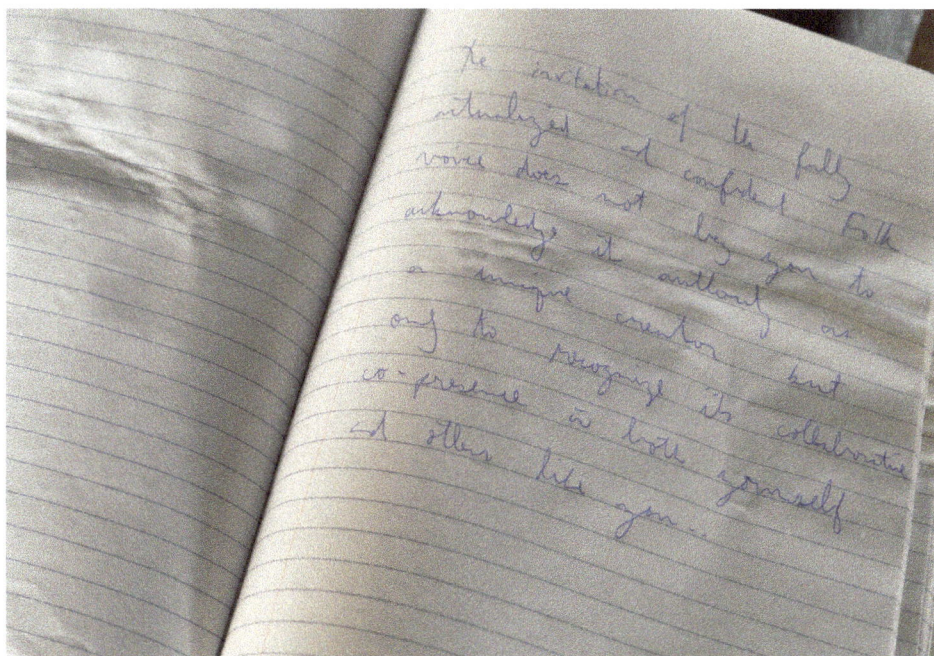

Detail from Henry Adam Svec's *Retracing Edith Fowke's Folk,* Montreal, 2011.

after the author's seminal work (1993). Is it by chance, by clever design, or due to membership in a shared community of discourse that Latour's role as an ethnographer of science labs and his sensitivity to hybrid social and political forms resonate strongly with Ethnographic Terminalia?

Kirkpatrick's own meditation focused on the question of what art is today, as he evoked competing art histories and the varying role of museums as commanding temples or forums of open communication and grassroots occupation. His piece was provocative for its visual intricacy and its "full" narrative, which was greatly enriched for this viewer by hearing the artist discuss his work. This experience pointed to the challenge of opacity in much contemporary art, an issue that is mirrored in critiques leveled against theoretically-dense ethnography that can seem inaccessible to some audiences. For many anthropologists, exhibiting their work in galleries is a form of public scholarship, an attempt to make their work more accessible. Yet art does not necessarily "speak for itself" and the pedagogical and affective power of hearing artists speak about their work should not be underestimated. The same can also be said of the process of witnessing others respond to art, which is a significant part of the sociality of gallery visiting.

Kirkpatrick's piece also alluded reflexively to "the museum," which became a kind of "fourth space" in Ethnographic Terminalia. A public discussion on research, ethics, and community led by Emelie Chhangur, Assistant Director and Curator of the Art Gallery at York University, introduced visitors to Vélez' more recent work, which resulted in a similar collaborative, choreographed, and highly-energetic spatial occupation of the Walker Court in the Art Gallery of Ontario by local First Nations and Toronto's Urban Runners (parkours).[7] Other pieces in Ethnographic Terminalia focused on exhibitions and self-display as tools for promoting public engagement. For instance, MomenTech's *International Public Space Library* displayed books with ex libris stickers pasted inside that invited visitors to take them. This is part of a global interactive project in which anyone can donate or take books wherever they are circulated. Siraj Izhar's T*ent X: Democracy Village, Parliament Square* presented crumpled sketches of slogans from the Occupy movement in London in an effort to evoke, in the artist's words, "the topology of signs at the encampment" as an inclusive, "post-political space." In these and other instances, the meaningfulness and politics of civic public space, as well as exhibitions, were amplified. Whereas the 2010 Ethnographic Terminalia in New Orleans was closely linked to post-Katrina local art activism, a similar sense of community engagement was lacking in Montréal.[8] It would have been enriching to include art that interacted with Eastern Bloc's mixed-income, culturally- and linguistically-diverse neighborhood, and its struggles against development and gentrification. Or, could there have been a gesture toward the nascent Occupy Montréal movement? Digital technologies and art making can document contemporary developments such as these much more quickly than traditional academic publications.

For contributors to Ethnographic Terminalia, Eastern Bloc Gallery offered an intimate yet public space to explore processes that are often hidden from view and clouded in mystique (those which take place in the lab and studio), or can become lost in translation (the dynamics of field experience which exceed academic texts). In response to the thematic of *Field, Studio, Lab*, contributors offered hybrid pieces that were conceptual, poetic, subtle, and fragmented – as well as documentary and activist-oriented. As an ensemble, the exhibition challenged not only textual anthropology, but also the notion of a pristine art gallery.

Notes:
1 See http://cerev.concordia.ca/, last accessed May 2013.
2 See http://ethnographicterminalia.org/, last accessed May 2013.
3 See http://incubatorartlab.com/, last accessed May 2013.
5 For more on the conceptualization of a humanities lab, see Hiatt (2005).
6 Ian Kirkpatrick, personal communication (April 7, 2012).
7 The Awakening Giigozhkozimin by Humberto Vélez was commissioned in conjunction with Humberto: Vélez: Aesthetics of Collaboration, Art Gallery of York University, 2011.
8 For more on Ethnographic Terminalia in New Orleans, see Brodine (2011).

References:
Brodine, Maria. "Struggling to Recover New Orleans: Creativity in the Gaps and Margins." Visual Anthropology Review 27.1 (spring 2011), pages 78-93.
Hiatt, Gina. "We Need Humanities Labs." Inside Higher Education (October 2005). http://www.insidehighered.com/, last accessed May 2013.
Latour, Bruno. "We Have Never Been Modern", translated by Catherine Porter. Cambridge: Harvard University Press (1993).

Humberto Vélez
The Fight
video
2009

The Fight is the culmination of a series of multidisciplinary workshops conducted by Panamanian UK-based artist Humberto Vélez. It documents a performance of five boxing matches staged inside the Tate Modern Gallery in London (2007). The project synthesizes boxing, dance, and music performance created in collaboration with three boxing clubs from Southwark, UK, and featuring music by Mc Mic Assassin, as well as choreography created by the dance company, Flawless. This project highlights the complexity of using popular cultural images and icons to create a new aesthetic language— one grounded in collaboration. Possibilities for understanding this expansion of the artistic are revealed through the juxtaposition of boxing matches, the music performances, and the dance choreography. The curators of Ethnographic Terminalia were also pleased to present a special screening of photographic documentation from *The Awakening* (2011)—a collaborative work Vélez produced in Canada with the Mississagua New Credit First Nations, the Monkey Vault Gym and Parkour artists, and Art Gallery of York University curator Emelie Chhangur. Vélez's performance project explores the aesthetics and the ethics of collaboration, and was staged as an occupation of Walker Court within the Art Gallery of Ontario in late 2011.

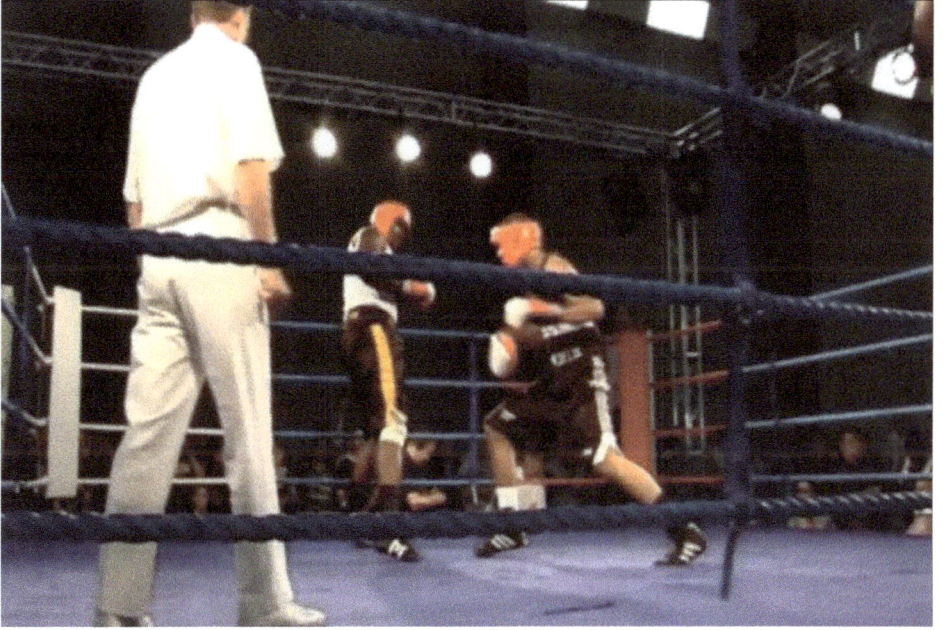

Ian Kirkpatrick
We Have Never Been Modern
digital print on cardboard
2011

A sculpture, a remix, and an interpretation: *We Have Never Been Modern*
brings together themes and ideas central to the projects included
in Ethnographic Terminalia 2011. The sculpture was the result of
an invitation by the curators to produce an artwork that responded
to the other juried works in the exhibition. Kirkpatrick's sculptural
collage draws together the permeable themes of field, studio, and lab
by highlighting relationships between geographical locations, iconic
artworks, signs, timelines, and ideas. On a scale model of the Tate
Modern, white figures stand out against an orange background, lined up
to represent Humberto Velez's procession into the Tate for *The Fight*;
place names reference physical locations in which artists generated their
work for Ethnographic Terminalia, such as Havana, Bilbao, London,
Paris and Montréal. This imagery is juxtaposed with poetic fragments of
description of works ('two musicians performed alone') alongside images
of Bourgeois' spider, the sphinx, musical scores, and diagrams. *We Have
Never Been Modern* refers to Bruno Latour's well-known rumination on
the dualistic split between nature and society; the very inseparability of
the works within the sculptural montage reflects this impulse. As the
artist writes, the "piece attempts to examine the larger networks within
which artistic inquiry operates—both today and in the past".

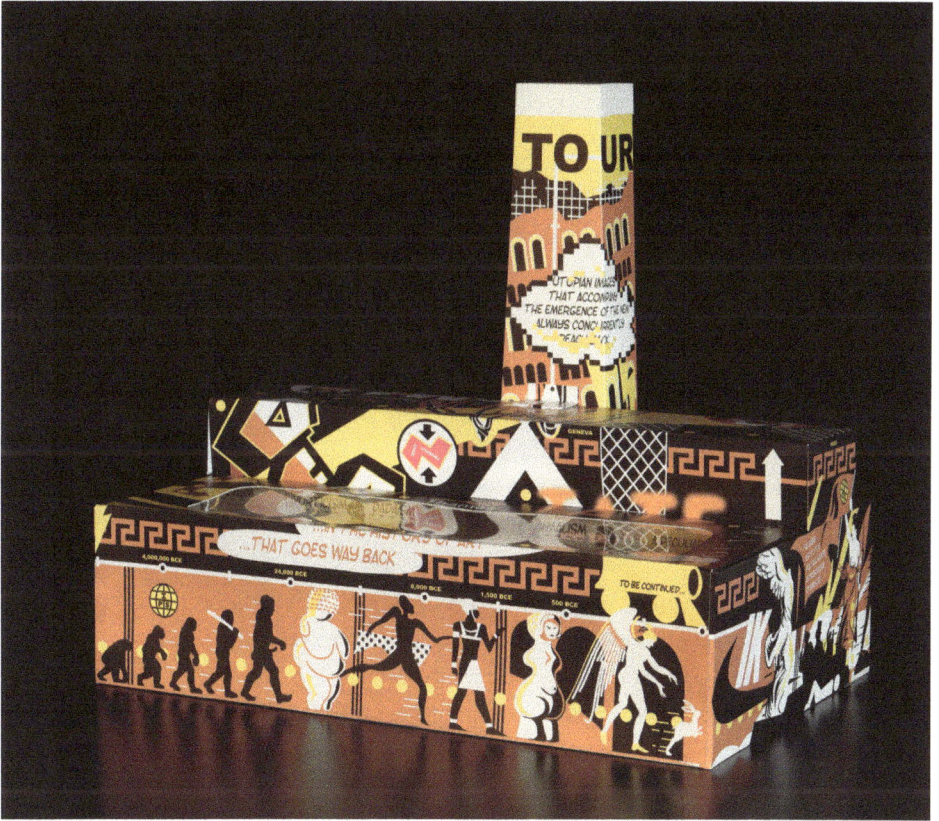

CEREV

Individual works: Erica Lehrer; Florencia Marchetti;
Monica Eileen Patterson; Joseph Rosen.
Student groups: Selina Antonucci, Ashley Clarkson
& Katie King; Matthew Foster, Florencia Marchetti,
Rachel Rotrand & Alejandro Yoshizawa.
video; audio; mixed media
2011

As Erica Lehrer, writes, "The Centre for Ethnographic Research in the Aftermath of Violence (CEREV) is a digital curatorial workshop at Concordia University that facilitates critical experimentation with exhibition practice and public cultural production around 'difficult knowledge.'" Curated by Ethnographic Terminalia in its own space within the gallery, the CEREV works represent research-in-progress, playing with the boundary between cultural research, studio and laboratory practice, artistic exhibition. Projects offer challenging new approaches to the Israeli-Palestine conflict, Argentinian political repression, South African apartheid, Jewish heritage tourism in Europe, and narratives of Holocaust memory. Collectively these works demonstrate the pioneering of the ethnographic media lab as a space of intercultural dialogue and aesthetic, and communicative experimentation.

Curating Difficult Knowledge

works-in-progress

EXHIBIT

How do we convey the
experience of violence?

What does it mean to curate
traumatic memory?

How do communities make
sense of, or make use of,
their tragic histories?

Renée Ridgway
Amish Country (the making of a quilt) and **Pennsylvania Dutch Quilt**
video; textiles
2009

As the artist writes, "Coming from a new world culture, history as a concept has always interested me—who writes it and who tells it. Using artistic means: in-situ, site-specific, materials, symbolic reference, new media, videos etc., I create installations that re-examine the construction of one or more identities in relation to specific spaces and places, re-examining the influence and manufacture of a historicizing simulation of past events through archives, oral testimonies and visual materials." This multimedia installation consists of a handmade quilt commissioned by Ridgway, installed alongside a single channel video installation entitled, *Amish Country (the making of a quilt)*. The video documents the dynamic collaboration between Ridgway and an Amish family, Jacob and Anne Esh. The design and construction of the quilt includes the combination of elements from both Dutch and American flags, reflecting Ridgway's cultural background.

Jennifer Willett
BioARTCAMP
photographs, badges
2011

BioARTCAMP navigates boundaries between lab and field-based scientific methodologies, toppling the discrete categorization of life by bringing lab specimens and 'natural' life forms into physical and conceptual proximity. Originally a large collaborative art/science project hosted in July 2011 by Jennifer Willet from INCUBATOR: Hybrid Laboratory at the Intersection of Art, Science and Ecology at The University of Windsor, and The Banff Centre for the Arts, *BioARTCAMP* was manifested as a variety of artists, scientists and students built a portable BioARTlab in Banff National Park, Canada. The project draws art and science, field, studio, and lab into one proximate location. As the artist writes, at "*BioARTCAMP* we traced 'explorer' and 'natural science' narratives from early explorers in the Canadian Rocky Mountains (and international figures like Jacques Cousteau) as applied to the context of contemporary biotechnologies". Ethnographic Terminalia hosted documentation of this site-specific inquiry through a series of photographic documentations framed with material traces of badges and memorabilia from the camp.

Benjamin Funke
One
video
2010-2011

Popular music and fandom are examined in this case study of the musical group Metallica versus the online music sharing service Napster®. By mining YouTube for performances of Metallica fans playing the song "One", Funke re-uses pre-existing digital footage, "molding and remixing material, multiplying its use and creating a new language within an existing language". Through engagement with this material, Funke delves into the world of copyright infringement, "stealing identifiable data off the internet, offering no financial compensation whatsoever to the rightful owners. This problem was initially brought to the public discourse by the mega-popular metal band Metallica, challenging their fans that were illegally downloading data files containing MP3's of the band's music. The band began a lawsuit against music trading website Napster®, saying that people would have to pay to listen to their music, and that it was not free. This lawsuit was inevitably targeted at their fans, their devoted followers. And the fans lost."

Chantal Francoeur
From radio to audio while exploring journalistic formats
MP3 sound work
2011

The effects of media convergence are explored in this original audio ethnography that highlights shifting broadcast mediums and journalistic cultural practices. As the artist writes, "Radio reporters collect field sounds, ambient sounds, rich silences and oral discourses. They put them together in order to tell a story, to create an impression. While this is an organic experience for both the reporter and the audience, media convergence changes that organic moment." The artist, a former radio reporter, creates a three and a half minute collage of voices and ambient sounds highlighting various journalist's worries about the loss of radio journalism and radio-rich personality. While exploring this topic, Francoeur uses the art of mixing and remixing the voices to proposes a new journalistic format of audio art.

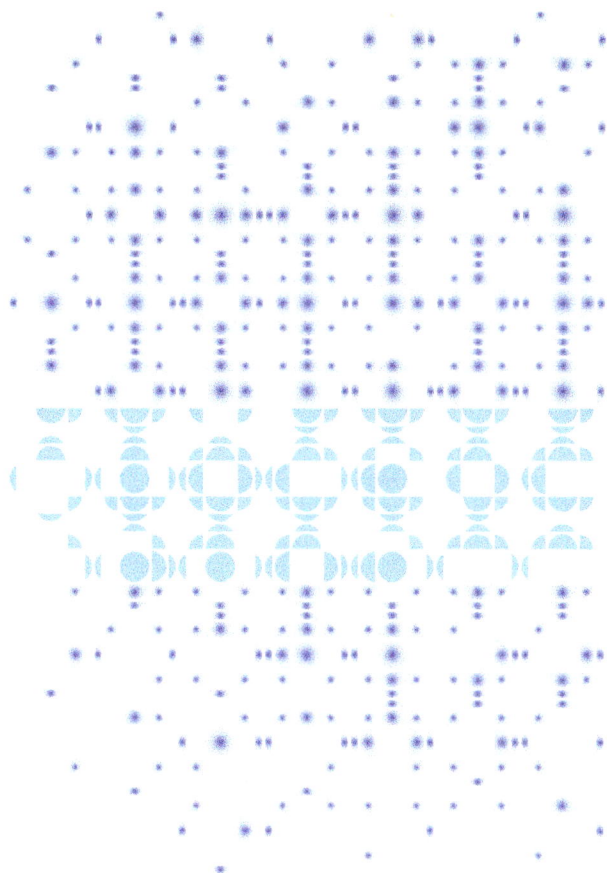

Venetia Dale
Touchmarks: The Social Life of Plastic Baskets
cast pewter from fragments of plastic baskets,
2009

The ubiquitous nature of the plastic basket and the precious sculptural form cast in pewter come together in Venetia Dale's *Touchmarks*. The work explores the social life of these transnational, mobile objects. The artist first became interested in plastic baskets while traveling in Southeast Asia in 2007. Dale writes, "Arjun Appadurai's examination of the life of an object, activated through the agent of exchange provided a framework in my own articulation of the social and cultural significance of this mundane object. In this series, I imagined a 'social life', a use, and a resulting form for these baskets exhibited here as *Touchmarks: The Social Life of Plastic Baskets*. The *Touchmarks* are the stamps found on historical pewter wares that designate guild, quality and authenticity of the wares. The artist has cast the contemporary product regulation (eg. made in India) into the pewter basket forms. In this way she provides a "new context for the distance between producer and consumer to be recognized and contemplated."

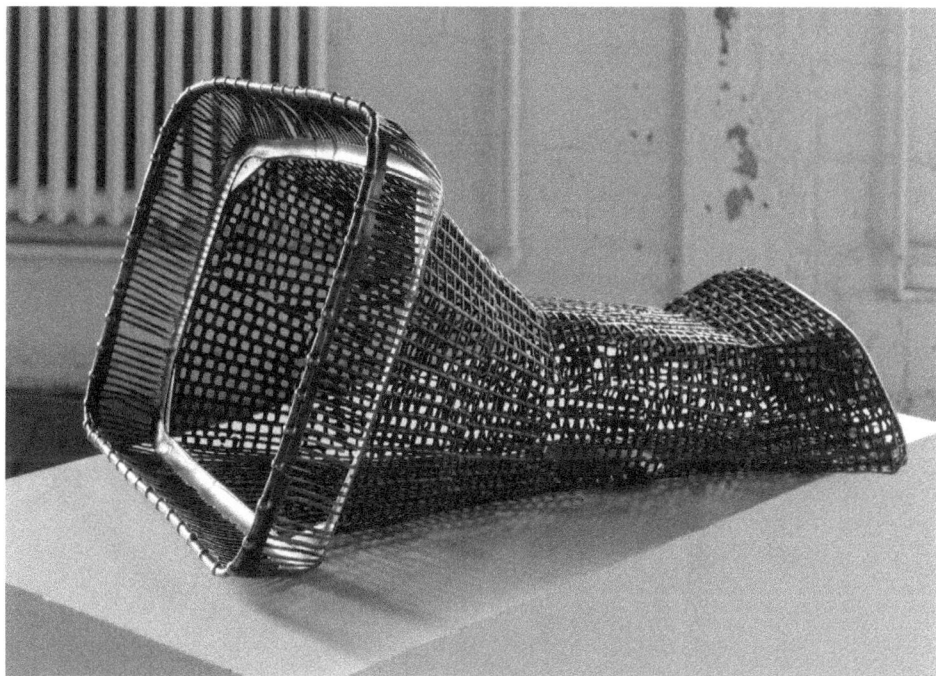

Barbara Rosenthal
International Garbage
video
2010

International Garbage is an experimental video documentary that
juxtaposes waste and consumption practices in Bejing, Paris, Moscow
and New York, with an audio intervention by the young German
sound artist Brandstifter. Installed as an intimate screening of the video
with headphones, viewers watch the split screen comparison between
practices to find that the video works, as Rosenthal points out "both as
abstract composites and as separate little movies charged and invested
with hidden meanings and commentary. What could that be? Look
again into your rubbish: seek hidden priceless gems. See what they tell
you about yourself and your culture; see what the method of collection
tells you about the same."

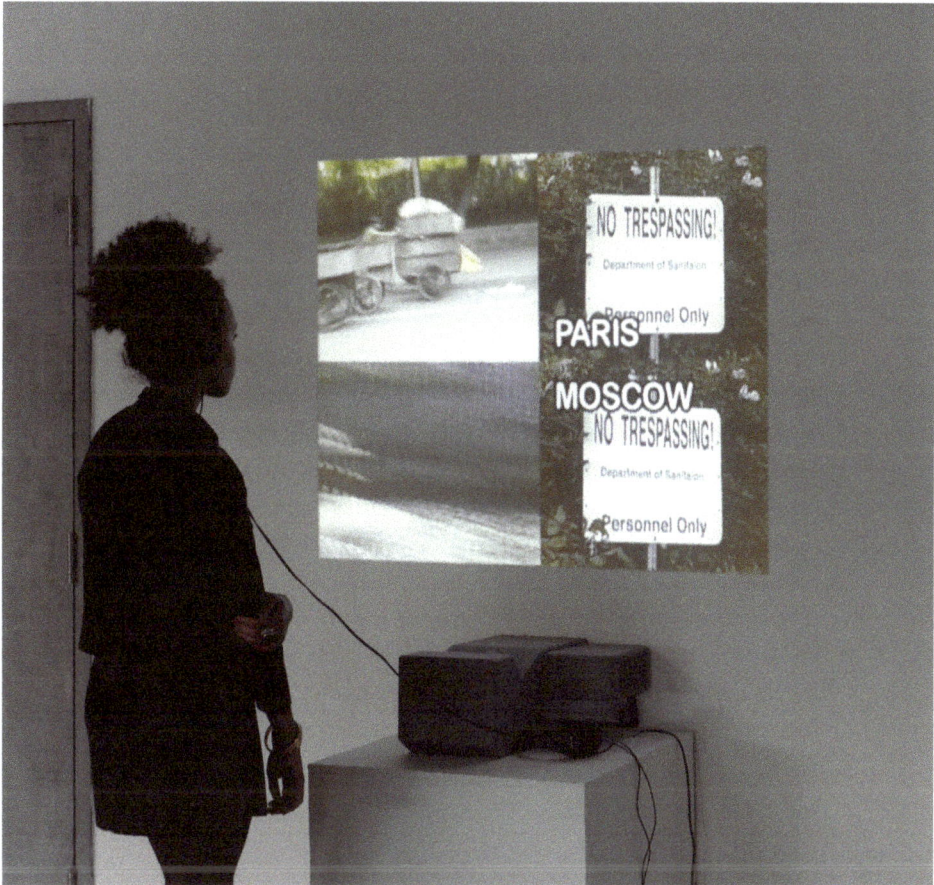

MomenTech
International Public Space Library
books and ex-libris stickers
2011

International Public Space Library (IPSL) is a global interactive library to which books are donated, given an IPSL ex-libris plate, and deposited for borrowers in a new and different public space—in this case, the gallery. Ethnographic Terminalia hosted IPSL within the gallery where, over the course of the exhibition, books about anthropology and art were brought together with books provided by the artists, such as those written by D.H. Lawrence and Valclav Havel. Visitors to the gallery browse through the library collection and select one to take with them, or add one to the library. After engaging with a book from the IPSL, the visitors are encouraged to deposit it somewhere in the public realm for a new reader to "borrow". Within the IPSL, anyone can either donate or borrow a book from the gallery. In addition to this, a stack of IPSL ex-libris plates allow people to affix them to other books and extend the library beyond the gallery. As the artists write, "IPSL explores how borders can be crossed—and ends can be turned into beginnings— simply by placing books in the public space".

Chantal Gibson
Historical In(ter)ventions: Altered Texts & Border Stories
mixed media
2010

Gibson challenges the myth-making of Canadian history by transforming existing books into containers for new representations of history. In the work _Historical In(ter)ventions: Altered Texts & Border Stories_ three black braided plaits frame the borders of a Canadian history book from 1935. Within the book, the artist has cut the pages to create a frame for a photo of a young Black girl, the artist's mother. A second sculptural bookwork entitled, _Book/mark_ hangs on an industrial chain installed from the gallery ceiling to greet the viewer at eye level; comprised of 2,978 bookmarks, this work is hand-cut, painted, and bound with jute in order to mark the historical _Book of Negroes_—a handwritten, military ledger containing the names and details of nearly 3000 Black Loyalists who came to Nova Scotia from the USA in the late-1790s. Gibson explains that "Promised land and freedom, lack settlers, the last to receive land grants, worked as slaves and indentured servants to survive. Privileging texture over text, _Book/mark_ offers alternative ways of reading this African-Canadian experience."

Andrew Norman Wilson
Toy Boat Task
video, Paper
2011

As a reversal of the normative outsourcing workflow between India and
America, *Toy Boat Task* represents the material traces of collaboration
and communication between the artist, Andrew Norman Wilson,
and his "virtual" personal assistant, Akhil. Email exchanges between
Wilson and Akhil are displayed on a table along with a model toy
boat built by the artist. A TV monitor loops a video made by Akhil
that documents the boat in India, in situ in the field, as he launches
it into a body of water. Sitting down at the table to read through the
email correspondence developed in the production of this piece, one
learns how the artist initiated a relationship with Akhil in Bangalore,
India through a virtual personal assistant service knowns as *Get Friday*.
Wilson notes: "I asked Akhil what he wishes he could be doing at work
– he said electronics and engineering. So we decided that he would
design a construction manual for the boats he used to make. I gathered
the necessary materials and have been building toy boats according to
Akhil's instructions. I sent him one of the boats in the mail, so that he
could make use of it."

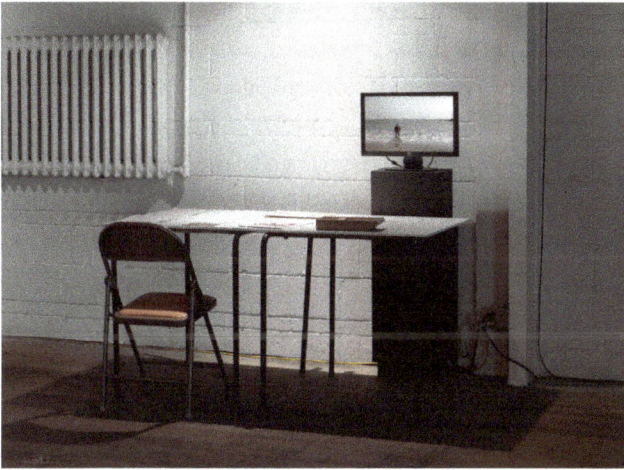

Steven Foster
Re-Mediating Curtis: Toy Portraits
light boxes, 3D cardboard glasses
2011

Stephen Foster's work *Re-Mediating Curtis: Toy Portraits* addresses
ongoing questions of Indigenous representation in popular culture.
Emerging out of a research project that uses interactive multi-media
and digital photo-based installation, this work takes up Edward Curtis'
ethnographic film, *In the Land of the Head Hunters* (later renamed *In the
Land of the War Canoe*), that was shot on Deer Island near Port Hardy
on Vancouver Island. As the artist notes, the film, and Curtis' other work
has been discussed at length in both anthropology and contemporary
art but little has been done to address the effect of his work on popular
images of Indigenous people. To this end, three lightboxes feature
portraits of plastic toys that represent stereotypes of Indigenous peoples,
a visual nod to Curtis' ethnographic photography. The lightboxes
reference commercial advertising displays for popular film promotion,
while the photographic portraits are created in 3D to reflect current
trends in commercial film production, particularly in films that represent
Indigenous cultures (such as James Cameron's *Avatar*).

Siraj Izhar
Tent X: Democracy Village, Parliament Square
paper, ink, crayon, cardboard box
2011

Text is embedded in paper folds of a crumpled piece of paper hanging
on the gallery wall: "After so many years...we still cry tears". Bright
marks, scribbles, and sketchy contours frame these words. The note is
part of a series of crumpled up dispatches that Siraj Izhar sent to the
curators from his field site at the Democracy Village encampment
at Parliament Square in the UK. The tent camp at Parliament square
was an improvised space made from improvised materials. Reporting
back from what the artist calls a "crumple zone", a post-political space,
the sketches are intended to translate the subjective experience of
the encampment and its topology of signs into an objective reality.
Each unfurled field note installed on the wall represents Izhar's
active participation and documentation of social processes. As the
artist writes: "they are about the making of new structures for human
experience, not only about producing representation. My working
philosophy has emerged more through practice, dialogue, and activism:
working with horizontal social networking, disseminating the work
through public workshops, 'infonights' at social centres, and self-made
zines/publications".

Henry Adam Svec
Retracing Edith Fowke's Folk
MP3 Sound Recording and field notebook
2011

In _Retracing Edith Fowke's Folk_, Henry Adam Svec draws together a diverse array of practices and media—folksong collecting, archival research, pseudo lectures, and fieldnotes—to ask "how does the documenter do justice to the immanent creativity of "the folk?" By staging a research project to retrace the steps of the late-Canadian-folklorist Edith Fowke, Svec's in-depth fieldwork and invitation to Canadian musicians, writers and artists to record Fowke's songs is given a strange twist. In what the artist stages as a mass-mediated hoax, Svec instead invites the artists to compose new songs with similar titles to those Fowke recorded in her day. Recorded in the field these songs are presented in the gallery as "fakelore" alongside fictional fieldnotes.

Public Laboratory for Open Technology and Science
Making Sense: Lab as Gallery as Field
site-specific installation
2011
www.publiclaboratory.org

In the course of the exhibition, the Public Laboratory for Open
Technology and Science (PLOTS) community turned the gallery into
a site of investigation to create *Making Sense: Lab as Gallery as Field*.
Using two low cost, Do-It-Yourself (DIY) tools to "create knowledge
about the composition of the environment, the materials within it and
the audience", the project introduces new modes of participatory science.
PLOTS is self-described as "a community which develops and applies
open-source tools to environmental exploration and investigation. By
democratizing inexpensive and accessible "Do-It-Yourself" techniques,
Public Laboratory creates a collaborative network of practitioners who
actively re-imagine the human relationship with the environment."
Combining a spectrometer and a hacked Roomba vacuum, Dosemagen,
Wylie, and their PLOTS collaborators created an original Roomba
Indoor Air Quality Monitoring device. Programmed to travel around
the gallery, the attached sensor and light system "result[s] in a tool to
assess sources of airborne pollution throughout an indoor space. During
[Ethnographic] Terminalia, [...] Roomba [is released] to map and study
the gallery space, generating data rich images on indoor air pollutants
such as Formaldehyde".

La Cosa Preziosa (Susanne Caprara)
Passa la banda?
MP3 recording, photograph
2011
www.lacosapreziosa.com

A single photograph on the wall hangs beside a set of headphones—
in the image, La Cosa Preziosa is captured making a field recording
of *Passa la banda?* in the village of Noepoli during the Festa di
Sant'Antonio on 11 June 2011. The title begs the question, "Is the
marching band coming by?" and marks the day when a religious festivity
approaches in this rural corner of southern Italy. As the artist explains,
the importance of the presence of la banda - sonically marking the
the occasion while also adding an air of celebration - is reassuring to
the community in its unchanging presence. *Passa la banda?* musically
highlights the passing of the Holy statue carried in procession- itself
a ritual marking of public space. In the gallery, listeners witness
instruments sonically distributed to be heard by as many people as
possible. This sonic experience is delivered with energy and amplified by
the narrow cobbled streets. The soundscape was composed specifically
for Ethnographic Terminalia and edits together the early morning
procession to the climax of the fireworks and tarantella dances. As
the artist writes, "this work represents the continuation in the artistic
exploration of the keynote sounds of my own cultural heritage. It also
raises the question of whether these sounds can speak to other cultures
listening in, and whether they translate as emotional expressions of
religious and civic sentiment".

Luc Messinezis
Eavesdropping Greece
wood, speakers, glass
2011
www.sonologik.com

This audio work depicts fights, conversation, lovemaking, and joy
recorded by an eavesdropper in urban Greece. The visitor to the gallery
mimics the embodied act of eavesdropping by pressing their ear against
a cup mounted to a faux wall. Luc Messinezis considers the work
within the realm of eavesdropping ethics. He writes, "Eavesdropping
though allows me to understand the events for what they are and
not for what they were supposed to be. Since these audible details of
everyday life were supposed to stay behind closed walls, I break the
rules, I bypass ethics and bring my ear close to the wall, listen and so
the walls have ears; my eavesdropper's ears."

Laura Malacart
Parliament
mixed media
2011

In *Parliament,* Malacart plays with Bruno Latour's (1993) idea of
a "parliament of things", in a photographic installation of close up
portraits of people. Troubling the relationship between subject and
collaborator, methodology and perfomance, the sitter for the portrait
looks into the camera with a hand—not their own—wrapped around
their chin in a typical photographic pose. Yet the face and hand belong
to different bodies. This creates an uncanniness and uncertainty in the
portraits, one that fluctuates between notions of collaboration and
intimacy, and threats of manipulation or abuse. As the artist writes, "The
unstable outcome of these collaborative performances becomes symbolic
of the instabilities of methodologies and the production of bodies of
knowledge."

Alyssa Grossman and Selena Kimball
Memory Objects, Memory Dialogues
double projection video
2011

This collaborative work between Alyssa Brossman and Selina Kimball combines two looped video projections playing simultaneously on opposing video monitors within an intimate private viewing room. One video features edited interviews comprised of recollections of Communist Romania and conducted by Grossman during her fieldwork in 2006-7. The Bucharest residents are featured sharing their memories and stories stimulated by Alyssa's collections of ordinary household objects that are associated with the period before the 1989 Revolution. The audio for the interviews are in Romanian with English subtitles. On the opposite wall, Kimball's film comprised of 16mm animations of these objects - seemingly banal items: an icecube tray, a torn sock, a wooden darning mushroom - "play as a contrapuntal dialogue between the artist, the anthropologist and the interviewees". Sounds of the animated objects play simultaneously with the audio of the interviews.

She turned it (on a lathe).

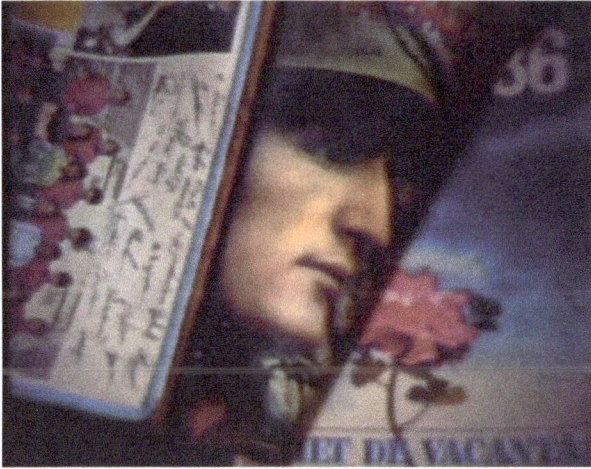

Alexandrine Boudreault-Fournier & Marie-Josée Proulx
Echo - The First Tie
double projection video
2010

"Tie (musical): Indicates that the two (or more) notes joined together are to be played as one note with the time values added together. To be a tie, the notes must be identical; that is, they must be on the same line or the same space."

Echo - The First Tie is a collaborative video and sound installation by anthropologist Alexandrine Boudreault-Fournier & artist Marie-Josée Proulx that features two musicians - one living in Montréal, one living in Cuba. In this complimentary double projection, the two musicians work together in a virtual space on an original music piece. The artist-anthropologists collaboration staged an encounter between the two musicians to induce a musical dialogue, "a relation, which allows a reflection on diasporic nostalgia". In a musical dialogue staged on two opposing video monitors installed in a darkened room, the sonic experience situates the viewer in the middle of this musical performance.

Sarah Christman
Broad Channel
video
2010

This short film from artist Sarah Christman explores the nuances of everyday activity over the course of one year along a public shoreline in New York City's Jamaica Bay. Over the course of four seasons the artist recorded a relationship between people, wildlife, and landscape that emerges on a "dirty strip of beach sandwiched between a landfill and JFK on Broad Channel Island". With over fifty hours of audio and 16mm film, the artist set out to show "[a] first encounter with this beach is both familiar and strange. It is a tenuous, evolving ecosystem, constantly in flux. People of all ages and ethnicities arrive and depart in waves, interacting with one another and their environment in seemingly commonplace ways— fishing, worshipping, scavenging, gazing. These human endeavors are carried out in parallel with the naturally occurring processes occurring above and below the surface."

Erin Newell
Letters from Frank: fff (fatima freedom fighters, not found family footage)
video
2011

A montage of standard 8 mm clips explores the artists' family's history as they traverse the Atlantic Ocean between Ireland and the United States. Artist Erin Newell edits together landscape images of America and Ireland to expose the differences and similarities in these images as they come up against her dual nationality. In a double screen shot through a circular lens, the artist overlays a recording of her own voice reading a list of moments and images that stand out to her within this personal history. Exploration of the personal archive, the enigma of family history, and the aesthetics of identity bring multisited fieldwork into the studio space.

Valentina Ferrandes
Lilong
video
2009

Lilong is a documentary collection of individual portraits and repetitive gestures contextualized by topographical images of a Shanghai community. Filmed in the People's Park, in the centre of Shanghai, Lilong is a settlement developed in Shanghai in the 1940s as a low-rise building with inner courtyards. A concern with the loss of the Lilong typology in contemporary Shanghai led the artist to film the peculiarity of Lilong: the interstitial spaces and the public and private life in the neighbourhood that is blurred and less defined than newly built estates and gardens. As the artist writes, "These 'openings' are so tightly integrated within the structuring of interiors in the dwelling, that life in the *Lilong* becomes characterized by an ambiguous relation between public and private sphere, as well as by a strong sense of neighborhood and cohesiveness...Public parks, People's Park in particular, are the beating heart of what is still visible of a traditional, public lifestyle, made of gatherings, singing, collective exercising, dance and play. While the urban and human geography of Shanghai is changing and mainly elderly people perform these activities, parks become also stages for fragmented "solo" performances".

Aryo Danusiri
The Fold
video
2008

Aryo Danusiri's video, *The Fold* is a record of the inside of a mosque in downtown Manhattan during the autumn of 2008. The artist investigates the relationships between religion, public spaces, and memory in contemporary American society. To answer "what does it mean to be a Muslim in Manhattan? What does it mean to be a "multicultural Muslim?" The artist films one long take of the routine of worship or leisure and "rhythms of folding and unfolding (act) as visual metaphor for the boundary between these seemingly disparate acts.... As its title alludes to, *The Fold* is a "song" of transformations in space and piety. Conceived as an investigation of the spatiality of religion and identity, the twist at the end of the work questions the boundaries between the spiritual and the mundane, the collective and the individual, the everyday and the political".

Lesley Braun
Blanche Neige: Live in Kinshasa
video
2009

In the summer of 2009, part of Lesley Braun's doctoral research was to perform as a dancer with a popular musical band in Kinshasa, Democratic Republic of Congo. The artist was interested in examining how lived experiences in an urban environment are communicated through movement and the ways in which female concert dancers are viewed and treated by society at large, and how they contribute and reflect the social imagination. The video shows the artist-anthropologist performing dance choreography as her research character Blanche Neige, or Snow White (a name given to her by the band). As the artist-anthropologist writes, "Through mimesis, though influences are absorbed, the individual nevertheless can retain his/her own identity without having to become whatever it is being imitated. In this way, dance as a participant-observation method has an ecstatic quality both in its inherent transcendence of the subject-boundaries, and in its performative aspects (Fabian 1985; Hastrup 1992)."

ETHNOGRAPHIC TERMINALIA:
2009-2010-2011

Shelly Errington, University of California, Santa Cruz

"Ethnographic Terminalia *is an exploration of what it might mean to exhibit anthropology—particularly in some of its less traditional forms—in proximity to and conversation with contemporary art practices.*"
    -Ethnographic Terminalia Prospectus.

Forty or 50 years ago, any anthology or book with the words "anthropology" and "art" prominent in its title was almost certainly devoted to anthropological theorizing about the works of formerly colonized peoples. No more, and not for a while.

Lately, anthropologists have been experimenting in new nontextual visual, aural, and plastic forms, and in digital pieces combining text, sound, and images (moving and still). Either alone or by collaborating with artists, they have been producing work that acts on the world, uses it, explores it, collaborates with it—in ways that may be evocative and thought provoking, sometimes politically charged, sometimes educational, and sometimes quite beautiful and intriguing to see or hear. Artists, for their part, have since the 1970s adopted materials and practices that may be reminiscent of participant-observation and ethnographic methods (and are often called that), or which may overlap with

Reprinted with permission. Errington, Shelly. Ethnographic Terminalia: 2009–10-11. American Anthropologist. 114(3): 538-542.

Facing page: general installation view, Montreal, 2011.

other anthropological preoccupations or subject matter. (On encounters between art and anthropology, see Schneider andWright 2006, 2010.)

The Curatorial Collective of Ethnographic Terminalia, an exhibition of Art and Anthropology, seeks to promote and encourage crossover works and experiments. ET has taken place as a temporary exhibit in conjunction with the annual AAA meetings in 2009, 2010, and 2011, and will take place again in 2012 in venues outside the convention hall but coordinated in the program through the Society for Visual Anthropology (see Figure 1). After the first exhibit, ET had local affiliates—Art Spill in New Orleans (2010) and CEREV (Centre for Ethnographic Research in the Aftermath of Violence) in Montréal (2011); the Curatorial Collective also invited known artists to "anchor" the exhibits prior to the call for submissions. And as of the third, the exhibits have themes: *Field, Studio, Lab* in 2011, *Audible Observatories* in 2012. Artist biographies and commentary can be seen on ET's well-designed and informative website (http://ethnographicterminalia.org).

Confronted with installations, multipaneled videos, mobiles, sculptures, photographs, listening stations, and more, under the rubric of "terminalia," some anthropologists will think of the end of anthropology as we know it, as in "terminal illness." The root of the word is actually Terminus, a boundary stone and the name of its associated minor Roman god. Ethnographic Terminalia is not about guarding boundaries, however: quite the contrary. From the ET website: "The terminus is the end, the boundary, and the border; of course the terminus is also a beginning as well as its own place, its own site of experience and encounter." The terminus stone here marks the place, the site, where the practices of art and anthropology cross, overlap, inform each other.

This sort of exhibit and others with compatible spirits but unlike subject matter (like the *Multispecies Salon* of 2010) are quite recent, at least in the context of the AAA meetings, and many anthropologists may not know it exists or may find it less intriguing than puzzling, or at best marginal (how appropriate that Terminus was a minor god, not one of the Pantheon!). It is certainly unusual in our profession and discipline, where most practitioners have historically aspired to achieve naturalistic representation and documentation. The forms may be unfamiliar, and not all the exhibited pieces were equally successful, in my opinion, as either "art" or as crossover ethnography or art (but then, how could they be?); but the themes of many of the pieces resonate with anthropological topics and concerns.

For instance, Susan Hiller, an installation artist who has studied archeology and linguistics, was one of the artistic "anchors" in 2010. She produced *The Last Silent Movie*, which "opens the unvisited, silent archives of extinct and endangered languages to create a composition of voices that are not silent" (from the ET website). Ryan Burns, another "anchor" (2010) showed *Profane Relics: an ossuary of the Congolese mineral wars*, a ten foot square block of red soil from which plaster casts (same color) of the detritus of an archeological matrix might emerge, including skeletons, cell phones, and laptops. In a more playful vein, the wellestablished artist Michael Nicoll Yahgulanaas presented *Seduction*, ten graphic panels showing a tale about Raven, and the short film *Red* (2009), about his graphic novel *Red: Haida Manga,* which tells Haida stories in (Japanese) Manga style.

Others reflected anthropological theorizing or topics even more directly. In the first year (2009) Trudi Lynn Smith's installation *Portable Camera Obscura* was fully within the purview of anthropological concerns: she deals with what she calls "iconic landscapes" in Canadian national parks and the ways they form the subject of different kinds of images, whether postcards, tourist snapshots, or government documents. Likewise, Craig Campbell's installation (2009) *Mobile Agitational Cinema: Iteration no. 1* (in spite of its frighteningly arty-sounding name) was a purpose-built mobile cinema that represents those made in the 1920s by communist agitators in Siberia, with footage that invites the visitor to reflect on the situation. Less dramatic but completely comprehensible to anthropologists was Chantal Gibson's *The Braided Book*, amixed media sculpture based on a 1935 textbook on Canadian history; Gibson cut out the text and replaced itwith a picture of a young black schoolgirl (her mother, she tells us) as a comment on what's left out of conventional history (see Figure 2).

Video art, websites, and soundscapes presented nonfiction with innovative twists or with breaks with naturalism and with our narrative presuppositions in ways that intrigued and attracted (see Figure 3). Stephanie Spray offered footage of a child in Nepal performing repetitive household chores and, another year, tea pickers going about their work—all without beginnings, climaxes, or endings. A video of a Holocaust survivor (by a group from CEREV) who educates by giving public lectures shocks by the routinization of his speech. An experimental video (by Florencia Marchetti) of the Argentinian disappeared explored place and memory. A video piece on garbage (by Barbara Rosenthal) juxtaposed simultaneous video of four cities' garbage disposal in four quadrants of the screen. *Elsewhereness*, by anchor artists Robert Willim and Anders Weberg, by contrast, played on sonic and visual stereotypes and riffed critically on site-specific sound art by assembling material about New Orleans from the web. La Cosa Preziosa's *Pasa la Banda?*, a soundscape of a Southern Italian town's religious event, was presented starkly without context in ET 2011 but is delightful on ET's website presented with a picture and a clickable audiofile.

The greatest outburst of art was in New Orleans, where Hurricane Katrina (2005) and the BP oil spill in the Gulf (2010) provoked a lot of art production, on view at both ET and Art Spill, the local partner that year. I was especially taken with the performance art–political protest and environmental art that year. I was heartened to read about the newly formed Krewe of Dead Pelicans, which puts on protest parades. (Krewes are the social clubs that put on Mardi Gras parades, and pelican is the state bird.) Maria Brodine (2011) provides an excellent theoretical exposition about Art Spill.

Some reviewers, and certainly some visitors, complained gently or loudly about the "lack of context" of the pieces. In fact, these highly theorized pieces are (sometimes) made comprehensible if one reads about them beforehand on the website. The greater obstacle to comprehension, however, is that theories are sometimes embodied within the artwork themselves, something anthropologists are usually not tuned into. In an interview, the anthropologist Steve Feld (2010:124) talked about the work itself as a form of theory: "The more I work with art, and with artists, and try to migrate the sensuous materiality of sound and image and object into zones of anthropological knowing, the more I encounter this kind of academic fundamentalism, like when people say, 'that was very poetic, but you didn't theorize the material.' What is to be done about anthropologists reducing theory to the literal, anthropologists refusing the possibility that theory gets done in all media and in multiple ways, including

Facing page: general installation view, Montreal, 2011.

artistic assemblage, performance, exhibition?"

At this point I want to speculate on what strands in both art and anthropology resonate with ET or havemade this type of exhibit intellectually, technologically, and imaginatively available, therefore enabling it to come into being.

First, "Art." For several centuries, while the so-called Renaissance Canon was indeed the canon and then for a century or more afterward, collectors and curators favored the acquisition and exhibition of framed, silent, durable, autonomous, commodifiable objects. To count as art, objects had to be stripped of ritual and of audience interaction, and were, above all, serious. Such objects continue to be the purview of what the art historian James Elkins (2002) calls "Normal Art History," whose moves are periodization, categorization, and authentication. If your idea of "art" accommodates only with the kinds of objects that are on display at major museum blockbusters featuring either treasures or masterpieces, then the works in ET will be as incomprehensible as "art" as they are as "anthropology," even at the borderlands.

In contrast to those silent and durable art works of yore, "Contemporary Art" dates from around 1960, when it exploded into the landscape of Art with Happenings, Installations, Conceptual Art, Maintenance Art, Fluxus, ... By now, in the 21st century, the rubric can cover a vast territory: Environmental Art, Social Architecture, Interventionist Art, New Genre Public Art, Site-Specific Public Art, Community Art, Participatory Art, and more. Several of those genres were on view at the ET exhibits. A nice sentence that points toward a very big strand of recent (this century) contemporary art practices was written by the French art critic Nicolas Bourriaud, who defines "Relational Aesthetics" as "a set of artistic practices which take as their theoretical and practical point of departure the whole of human relations and their social context, rather than an independent and private space" (Bourriaud 2002:113). That gestures toward a lot of heterogeneous events and practices.

The practices are heterogeneous, but, to state some of the basics: contemporary arts tend to collapse a distinction between "high" and "low" art (unless they are subverting it, in which case the separation is maintained but is inverted or turned inside-out). Likewise, the distance between subject (viewer) and object

Facing page: detail of Public Laboratory for Open Technology and Science's *Making Sense: Lab as Gallery as Field*, Montreal, 2011.

(artifact) is collapsed, as the art piece may require embodied participation. They allow multiple points of view or ways into the art object–process–performance. They may build or promote socially useful projects or make interventions to expose injustice or power relations. They may try to provoke and problematize. The artist may relinquish the role of auteur, becoming a facilitator, organizer, or enabler. The concept may be more important than the final object, if indeed there is one; hence, they are often highly theorized. Likewise, the "work" may be the process, hence temporary, performative, or ephemeral. That can make commodification and display in a gallery difficult. To be recuperated as objects and therefore be available to galleries, curators, and art historians, they may be filmed or photographed, or presented as a blueprint ormodel, or even as a record of what the artist did: hence, the displayed "object" in the gallery is not the work of art: it asserts, rather, it is a record of what happened or is a model for what could happen again. Some may be parodies or commentaries on conventions and art movements, and some, although apparently playful and good spirited, are made with extremely serious intent. A lot of artists are doing a lot of things in lots of places; they may resonate with each other, but it is difficult to imagine them as happening in the line of art–historical time or as a march of great artists and influences going in one direction. The world, in these kinds of arts, is less "represented" than it is engaged, exposed, and worked on.

Anthropology's ancestral heritage has more in common, metaphorically, with the Renaissance Canon than with Contemporary Art; it has historically favored the style of optical naturalism in visual imagery, the voice of the sober objective narrator in texts removed from the observed world, the construction of the reading or viewing subject as passively receptive and disembodied. And, just as historically most museum art has been in a frame or on a pedestal, rendering it an autonomous and movable object outside the world it depicts, our ethnographies in the form of texts stand as autonomous objects, enclosed physically with front and back covers and delimited as narratives by beginnings and conclusions.

A question might well arise, then, as to how anthropology could possibly intersect with contemporary art practices. My thought is that the ground was prepared by the late 20th century crisis in the humanities about representation but that developments in visual anthropology allowed an epistemological break.

Facing page: detail of Siraj Izhar's
Tent X: Democracy Village, Parliament Square, Montreal, 2011.

AFTER SO MANY
YEARS..... WE STILL
CRY YEARS

The general crisis of humanities and social sciences in the 1980s and 1990s shook up and transformed many of our naturalized assumptions about what ethnographic narrative and structure should or could be, opening up professional practices to experimentation in writing, to new categories of subject matter, and therefore to different thinking practices. The crisis problematized representation, signification, vision, reflexivity, the body, the politics of interaction, space and place, and almost anything else, and the rethinking continues.

Visual anthropology, a subfield, was of course affected. During most of the 19th and 20th century, photographs had been used in the profession as proofs, as examples, as demonstrations, as research tools, and as documents. In the last 20 years, though, photographs have moved from being used as research tools to being topics of study in their own right, launched with the 1992 publication of Elizabeth Edwards's edited *Anthropology and Photography: 1860–1920*. Firmly within the spirit of Colonial Discourse studies, it had the galvanizing effect of problematizing the transparency and "documentary" attributes of anthropological photographs and even "vision." Close to the same time, Paul Stoller (1989) argued, and Steven Feld's (1991) CD exemplified, an emerging professional urge to put embodiment and a sensorium broader than "vision" into ethnography (whether textual or filmic), and both came out at the cusp of the switch to digitizable media. Soundscapes and interactive media linked or linkable to the web could thenceforth be theorized as form of anthropological endeavor. (See also Feld and Brenneis 2004.) A few years later, visual anthropologist Peter Biella (1997) and filmmaker and ethnographer Roderick Coover (2003) produced CD-ROMs very different from each other in intent and genre but exploring the capacity of digital media to create densely informative and interactive ethnographic experiences.

Harvard's Sensory Ethnography Lab, founded in 2006, exemplifies all these trends; its purpose "is to support innovative combinations of aesthetics and ethnography, with original nonfiction media practices that explore the bodily praxis and affective fabric of human existence. As such, it encourages attention to the many dimensions of social experience and subjectivity that may only with difficulty be rendered with words alone" (from the website). Canada (where several of the core ET curators have roots) has many such centers and schools, with names featuring phrases like, for example, Simon Fraser's School of Interactive Arts + Technology. In short, digital media allows and encourages potentially far more than "visual" matter or methods.

Crossover works of anthropology and art like some on display at ET and many other current experiments have their roots in what Sarah Pink (2011) calls "Digital Visual Anthropology." It is, Pink writes in 2011, "still in its infancy," but she points to many of the possibilities opened by digital media. Although the roots are in DVA, I think I'd call these ET and related works something like "Digital/Intermedia Anthropology." They need not actually use digital technology, but the confluence of three developments makes DIA technologically possible. Those, in turn, make DIA imaginatively possible and prompt exploration of new forms of representation, intervention, and subjectivity.

The three key developments are the availability of digital media, of small affordable e-devices, and the Web. This confluence did not simply allow people to dowhat they had been doing before, but more easily: rather, it enabled a different attitude comprising an imaginative and even epistemological break. It is probably no accident that many of the Curatorial Collective and a number of the exhibitors in the ETs come out of or have connections to Digital Intermedia Anthropology in the largest sense—nonfiction experimental film and website constructions, collaborations via the webwith artists and with First Peoples and other communities, or public art projects that use e-devices to educate the public that contain audio files of ambient sound, narrative, and images. Many of the exhibitors are interested in spaces and how bodies move through them and the kinds of subjectivities that are constructed as the user (I use that word, rather than "viewer" or "audience") moves in and out of the works and the spaces and places they occupy or gesture toward. These works may be "interactive" but not necessarily digitized. They all strive to be nonfictional. Many are playful, intentionally provocative, or evocative. None tries to "represent" in a naturalistic way; they are seldom about making truth claims, although they may try to provoke the user into thinking about truths.

The works in ET will probably never replace textual ethnographies. But the exhibit is a fascinating multidimensional portal through which we can enter and learn about experiments in thought and technology that intrigue, amuse, and may even inspire us to attempt new forms for our own nonfictional works.

Note Acknowledgment. Thanks to Jennifer Gonzalez for conversation and a reading list and to Arnd Schneider for a once-over of a draft of this review.

References

Biella, Peter
    1997 Yanomamo Interactive: The Ax Fight (CD-ROM). With Napoleon A. Chagnon and Gary Seaman. Fort Worth: Harcourt Brace.
Bourriaud, Nicolas
    2002 Relational Aesthetics. Dijon: Les Presses du Re'el.
Brodine, Maria T.
    2011 Struggling to Recover New Orleans: Creativity in the Gaps and Margins. Visual Anthropology Review 27(1):78–93.
Coover, Roderick
    2003 Cultures in Webs: Working in Hypermedia with the Documentary Image. Imprint Watertown, MA: Eastgate Systems.
Edwards, Elizabeth, ed.
    1992 Anthropology and Photography, 1860–1920. New Haven: Yale University Press in association with the Royal Anthropological Institute, London.
Elkins, James
    2002 Stories of Art. New York: Routledge.
Feld, Steven
    1991 Voices of the Rainforest. Program Notes by Steven Feld. Imprint Salem, MA: Rykodisc.

Feld, Steven, in conversation with Virginia Ryan

 2010 Collaborative Migrations: Contemporary Art in/as Anthropology. In Between Art and Anthropology: Contemporary Ethnographic Practice. Arnd Schneider and Christopher Wright, eds. Pp. 109–126. Oxford: Berg Publishers.

Feld, Steven and Donald Brenneis

 2004 Doing Anthropology in Sound. American Ethnologist 31(4):461–474.

Pink, Sarah

 2011 Digital Visual Anthropology: Potentials and Challenges. In Made to Be Seen: Perspectives on the History of Visual Anthropology. Marcus Banks and Jay Ruby, eds. Chicago: University of Chicago Press.

Schneider, Arnd, and Christopher Wright, eds.

 2006 Contemporary Art and Anthropology. Oxford: Berg Publishers.

Schneider, Arnd and Christopher Wright, eds.

 2010 Between Art and Anthropology: Contemporary Ethnographic Practice. Arnd Schneider and Christopher Wright,eds. Pp. 124. Oxford: Berg Publishers.

Stoller, Paul

 1989 The Taste of Ethnographic Things: The Senses in Anthropology. Philadelphia: University of Pennsylvania Press.

www.ingramcontent.com/pod-product-compliance
Lightning Source LLC
Chambersburg PA
CBHW040138270326
41927CB00020B/3437